Landscape of The Wait

poems by

Jami Macarty

Finishing Line Press
Georgetown, Kentucky

Landscape of The Wait

Copyright © 2017 by Jami Macarty
ISBN 978-1-63534-235-2 First Edition
All rights reserved under International and Pan-American Copyright Conventions.
No part of this book may be reproduced in any manner whatsoever without written permission from the publisher, except in the case of brief quotations embodied in critical articles and reviews.

ACKNOWLEDGMENTS

Grateful acknowledgement is made to the following publications in which some of these poems appear:

Grain: "1st Dream Since," "2nd Dream Since"

Slant: "Aground"

These poems have been supported by the kind hearts, willing ears, and generous pockets of the following poets and organizations. I am deeply grateful to the Community of Writers at Squaw Valley and 2010 mentors Kazim Ali, Forrest Gander, and Dean Young, who loved me through the first week of the accident and the fractal beginning of these poems; to British Columbia Arts Council for funding my 2014 proposal to write a poetic response to the accident; to Banff Center's Writing Studio and 2015 mentor Tim Lilburn for holding space as the fragments found form; to Omnidawn Publishing's "Prosody & Revision" course and its teachers, especially: Rusty Morrison and guests: Norma Cole, Gillian Conoley, and Donald Revel for their attentive readers' responses.

Thank you:
Edward T. Mahoney, my Uncle Eddie (June 3, 1927 – September 25, 2010)
Mary M. Mahoney, my Auntie Mame (July 23, 1931 – March 6, 2016)

Publisher: Leah Maines

Editor: Christen Kincaid

Cover Art: Jerry N. Uelsmann

Author Photo: Vincent Wong

Cover Design: Link Nicoll

Printed in the USA on acid-free paper.
Order online: www.finishinglinepress.com
also available on amazon.com

Author inquiries and mail orders:
Finishing Line Press
P. O. Box 1626
Georgetown, Kentucky 40324
U. S. A.

Contents

1   Fracture
11   Alteration
12   Landscape of The Wait
13   At the Time of Accident
14   1st Dream Since
15   Aground
16   Small Turned Needs
17   Sisters
18   Two Strains
19   Variables
20   New Vocabulary
21   Three Months
22   Ejected
23   2nd Dream Since
24   Related
25   Dear World
26   Winter Field
27   3rd Dream Since
28   Dear William
29   4th Dream Since
30   Reconstruction
32   If Only What If

This book is written in honor of William, my beloved nephew.

Fracture

where I pull over   to listen to
                                 the desolate
cellular voice

a hummingbird   needles weeds
invading   the clear felling

where pell-mell interstate   his body
                                 through the car window
happens happens happens

where the family   paces waiting's room

where *do you think*   has no application

where our questions   asked
in this fold   of universe
can only be answered   in his

where the fractured   glimpse
                                 the eternal

where a son matters   more than ever
                                 to his mother

~

Where in my choice and forcing a chair
into the exact shade   luxury

William   where
in ICU   comatose

~

how many more words   can be gotten into this day

no change the update said   abnormal response

that's thinking   or
is it

where's the feeling   of it being early yet

let him take his time

~

where the other side of the other side of
aspen leaves
turn silver to the sun

where his mother turns a cup in her hand

maybe the body does make sense

today no different from yesterday

push the soup away   recharge the phone

~

where my eyes see   gradient ridge

pines' staggering height

will his eyes

~

 where tonight   fireflies

 hurry a field

 retrospective   blue to black dusk

 where bats lord near barn

          Mystery Saints

 what took him from our causeway of cells

~

 where truth can go different ways

 what calculus of logic   explains

 in each car and body

 the potential for crash

~

three suns   where

east   west

no change   no change

no change

~

row sweet William
                    row back to us

outwater the water

~

where the sky earlier   tried fierceness

out of darkness   the fanged rictus of stars

field's transformed   by overturned car

hideous bloom flying through

music he wanted to listen to

                                   can we know his song

~

life transfiguring flight where
                                  everything
depended on his landing
                                  body apart
from brain

median grass back-broken

under his dead weight

is he leaning into healing   or receding

~

where our eyes dim

where our minds fixate

                                          on what differences

Undershoveller of Bones

is it the lucky ones who live

is it

~

son   a shadowed Now

where days of no change   extend beyond

days   of change

~

hope   the shield of the wary

rummaging for what to do
                                  in inadequate light

we shouldn't rush certainty

where does *should* come from

~

where

him in presence   or absence

dusk   or dawn

~

where he is   out in the wild nothing

waving farewell

where he is   slipping from Gone even

where he is half way to

                           shall he ransom his death

~

were we fools to think he'd outlast us

we're where that's how it's *supposed* to be

may we not measure him

                           by what he did not do

where

                           or what he did

~

where rowing   in the river of God

he understands better than all of us

                                                short abundant canals

waiting to hold him

commend into our arms   his living dying

let us let him go   if he asks that of us

Alteration

Did you know when you woke this is the day
you'd swerve to miss the rogue semi tire
finding yourself against gravity and
logic ejected from your rolling car
More pressure in your skull than than than what
I don't know You don't know Do you Did you
        For weeks there's been the presence of something
bad's going to happen   Then we craze in
the what ifs   If only that 90-min
medivac unnecessary   That belt
clicked into into into the air of
your catapult goes my mind to inhabit with you
that alteration in the membranous fabric
        Here where we are where we wait
we have our reason to wait   and our wish
to do something ably   to act   That brand
of action that will allow us to meet
again again again at a Swasey Park
family picnic   Our world inside yours
let us separate the inversion of
your car from from from you   Suspended in
your healing sleep let us be in your dream
        What is a day like this   A waste   Would we
call it that   What worth will be conferred
future future future in the then then
which may not or is aqueducts

Landscape of The Wait

a code carriages
our vigil over his comatose form

he sleeps a week now
while we stay awake
in days of unnatural routines
overneeding evasion

wait
        monitor   when or ever

        time that milestones
our want
                his eyes to open

doubt large now
        breath or gravel

each instinct's
        trance

how *deficit* out paces
the part written bare
        when thought turns to his future

something statistical travails

At the Time of Accident

airborne, he thought. hang-
ing on time's lost line
suffer suspension,
he thought. near-sighted
horizon. *no or-
dinary flying
falling*, he thought. lain
unregainable
in median grass.
*reconsider mind-
lessness*, he thought. in-
jured language in his
left hemisphere, like-
ness thin, *ask to see
what's missing*, he thought.
sometimes *I decide*,
he thought, looking for
Friday, the ending
of the week or the
beginning of fast
lane of chance. tire
scree, a crumbling re-
cord. a slit of sky
holding the vessel.

1st Dream Since

Two sisters and their mother are in a leaky ship. It's morning and they're between showers, getting ready to go to the hospital. There are too many of them and the space too small. That is, to contain their *what's happened*. In the bathroom, water is coming from the walls and the toilet paper is wet, pulpy. One of the sisters, the mother of the injured boy, takes all quarter and is given it. She goes first, and the others give her that. That's important to her. For the others it's different, which is not the point. The son is elsewhere both in dreaming and waking. They're none of them ashore yet.

Aground

at maximum ebb—
how goes the world
that nonpurposefully
runs your ship aground

horizontal hulk afloat mud flat
lies across wind
a dissonance that is there
but we don't want it to be

alien afternoons the penalty
we don't know what you know

how about this aseptic room
you don't open your eyes in
every day swelling more tubes
tracheotomy questions

whose nurse's hands
these are on your genitals

how you are unbroken
beyond what this is

one day every day
we keep thinking we will wake
from this tanker, its conspicuous
gloom filling the center

and you won't be in that hospital bed
and the sea will be a magic again

Broken On Suddenly

we have felt the world shape
your limboed sling

neither grave
nor a yes

you fitting

to a point
or vastness

a kaleidoscope or
a single-hued land

continuous without
continuing

your elaborate brain

a cause of amazing
identity

hardly here

Sisters

I call her saying Sorry, I don't have anyone else to call

My favorite uncle's days from leaving his body

The feeding tube's removed

She says she feels like she's always a few steps away from falling off a cliff

Everyone else's life has gone on

Hers exists on a traffic island

The cars driving around her

She says she's a shell

Can't sleep, eat

She misses him, *my son*

What's bothering her is she cannot fix this, his coma

Then she corrects herself and says she can

By being there

And she is

Two Strains

ventilator like a mother
commands what the brain interprets

hoping for a rechargeable battery
or a better nothingness for you

do I dare bake bread
dream a dimension of what's possible

we don't see the leaves
fall and they fall whether
we see them or not

if when you extended
beyond driver's seat
you could have been dreaming

we all could have been dreaming

of safe harbor

Variables

we are all together and
you are not here

we are all together because
you are not here

      all variables equal X

building the house with Before's rooms
installing favorite windows of who you are
we're in the midst of holding on

thinking we know
the night to you is monstrous
we talk about what you could become

New Vocabulary

Atelectasis (right lower lobe)
Axonal Injury (extensive diffuse)
Basilar Skull
Bronchostomy
Communicating Hydrocephalus
Decerebrate Posturing
Epilepticus
Feeding Gastrostomy Tube
Glasgow Coma Scale
Hemicraniotomy
Heterotropic Ossifications
Hypoxemia
Inferior Vena Cava (IVC) filter
Intubated
Lacrimal
Midline shift
Methicillian Resistant Staph Aureus
Obtunded
Paronchia
Paroxysmal Instability with Dystonia (PAID)
Percutaneous
Septicemia
Tachycardia
Tracheostomy
Ventricular catheter
Ventriculoperitoneal shunt

Three Months

through the window orderlies turn your back

we're in the light of events

what light   what events

autumn's   a dark occupancy

regret's skeletal

your coma   speaks a fortress

call this a test

you've been arbitrarily excluded

what is this arbitrary moat

Ejected

space
full of black—

    black tire
    black asphalt

two dark lips
between which I collide

bang
my basilar skull

my brain shift of midline

becomes a place

 of will I am

a constellation of inquiry

a petition to God

2nd Dream Since

You did what they said you won't do. You woke up. You sat up from your hospital bed, dressed, walked out, and were driving me to the family picnic. I was concerned about where you would sleep because your mattress had been thrown away, wanted to explain what they did and why, that all of it was reversible or a detail. We'd find you a new place to sleep.

Related

      Some of us have our back to it.

His mother excludes others of us our upset.

      She excludes as mirror to her feeling excluded

and that's true.

      She can never be more related to her half-family.

His train laps 100 nights

      grails the missing neurological responses.

Now it seems it was never not this

      tracheotomy.

One theory of his gap in consciousness—

      he's an archivist in his stacks of sleep.

He maybe dreams of finding the map

      for enchanted reentrance

where every key fits its lock

      and the peaches are especially fresh.

Dear World

Morphine drip and not breathing for more than 30 seconds each minute, Uncle dissolves to sag and bone. Why couldn't he go in his sleep instead of while his wife of 50 years eats meatballs. She sits in his chair. TV on. Fingers crossed. As if we have control over how bumpy the ride. We're an untethered kite nosing west. Sure, there's a pilot. The rest is up to chance or unforeseen variables. We can know the reason, say, of no in-flight service. But how many events occurred before the boy's car collided with the semi's tire? There's long-term need that worries us. Trust in doctors, that's paramount. The sun on my face, closer at 37,000 feet. The boy has increased fluid on his brain ventricles, more than in the last CAT scan. So that's how this is going to go. Right parietal bone removed. Cerebral shunt.

Winter Field

Snowy white mimeos
Non-white
Ordering existence into place
Where we wait by walking.

Sky's a steward folding, unfolding
Half-tone twin to
Earth's resigned encompassing.
Exhalations scribe an air legend, map
Purpose in feet.

Barbed suturing
Arbitrates the possible union of
Rolling hills and
Body's pastoral
Entrée. Wire dismantles effort.
Distant sheep interlope.

Walking our hymn to motion, indefinite
Insistence. Hope
Reduces, husks behind us
Exposing every undoing bone.

3rd Dream Since

There's something loud coming through the foliaged trees. The Interstate traffic won't stop in two directions. Are you okay, a man asks. He's focused on the blood coming from your left ear and mouth, chaining your neck. A woman's hand over her mouth in the periphery. Her ear holding a phone. When I arrive you call to me—say goodbye.

Dear William

Hours climb into much atmospheric pressure and wind. Your Being, a quiet insistence, stays with us. What is actively? A fortuneteller looks for the right left swerves' meaning. Your father's leaving again. Your mother stays almost too much. The tire's screeching, an imagined memory. Your muscles' atrophy a reality. The doctors cause us to consider the caveat. At times when we want certainty, we are skeptical of your mother's faith. Six months ago all your words were rolled out of you. The fate of truck loose tire. Whose were the hands that didn't finish tightening those lug nuts? Of a sudden, you snatched out of the field. Even after all your trying, all your early rising, your having a job and a car—short range boy. Poor boy trapped in all our thinking. Thought is obstacle. Broken body you have, but is not you. You are completely safe and unharmed. Do I dare envy you your escape with the chips you have? Our youngest, our bravest, continuing takes disappearances—is that it?

4th Dream Since

The catapult promise of your body consumes onlookers' attention at the Interstate Fair. At the letter writing booth, I write: Dear Interstate, Cancel the intersection of black asphalt and black tire. The onlookers marvel at the oblong arc of you cannon-shot from car window. I rush to write another letter: Dear Ground, undo skin mapping the gravel grid, undo the unappeasable weight of body landing.

Reconstruction

Tire and asphalt have similar color hues on light spectrum so conspicuity of the tire becomes difficult.

A full tire rotating prior to Mitsubishi driver's avoidance would prolong his reaction and complicate the decision as to which way he should turn to avoid the tire.

With respect to trajectory, enhanced photographs show tire marks commence to the right, indicating Mitsubishi initially swerves to the right to avoid, then comes back across initial lane (3rd) before moving off to the center median.

2D photogrammetry shows the Mitsubishi moved approximately 175 to 200 feet in avoidance to rest.

Calculated speeds based on distances range from 60 to 70 mph.

Tire mark evidence depicts the front tires of Mitsubishi were in full lockup, the rear tires sliding outward as Mitsubishi moves counterclockwise to a full lateral movement with passenger's side leading.

Passenger side of Mitsubishi leads into the median.

Passenger side tires dig into earthen material and trip vehicle.

Passenger side roof rail sustains superficial abrasions as vehicle commences roll.

Roof abrasions do not extend over entire width of roof.

Mitsubishi has to have left the ground for no contact to occur in the middle of the roof.

Mitsubishi comes down onto the ground during a final roll sequence directly over driver's seated position.

The A-pillar collapses into the driver's seated position.

Even if seat-belted, driver can sustain a vertical compression of spinal cord, driver's head can make contact with pavement during roll sequence, driver can sustain virtually the same or similar types of contact to physical body as if ejected.

If Only What If

if only you hit *snooze*
what if mid-leaving you slow to feed your fish
if only one thousandth of a second
what if one billionth of a second
if only the car keys slipped between seats
what if the car's battery needed a jump start
if only you had drawn the safety belt
what if you lived closer to work
if only you took the back way
what if, approaching the toll booth, you pull over to search for change
if only your radio operative
what if the iPod had yet to be invented
if only the semi driver called in sick
what if he stopped for gas
if only inspected, the truck red-flagged
what if tire bolts fully tightened
if only having to dislodge, the tire halted in the median
what if neither you nor the truck driver traveled the fast lane
if only you slowed mid-air, life dialoguing with meaning
what if ladies and gentlemen, we're just in a bit of a holding pattern
if only tiny chapters of breathing on your own between ventilator
if only a swallow
if only a blink
if only a reflex
what if fragmented warning for a start of lower expectations
what if another spontaneous fraying into our survivor's guilt
if only instruction explained trauma to the frontal lobe
if only possible recovery scenarios
if only no caveats with extended footnotes
if only attentive to randomness, exception
if no matter the unlocking, day can become road scarring
if no one deserves this, certainly not you

www.ingramcontent.com/pod-product-compliance
Lightning Source LLC
LaVergne TN
LVHW050045090426
835510LV00043B/3232